Mama Prays
a 30 day devotional for Catholic moms

Samantha Stephenson

Copyright © 2022 Samantha Stephenson

All rights reserved.

ISBN: 9798818919218

DEDICATION

For my ever-patient Mother , thank you for never giving up. For my own mother, who taught me how to delight in my children. Thank you for your example. For Mommom, thank you for loving me like I was your own. See you soon, I hope (but not too soon!).

CONTENTS

	Acknowledgments	i
1	Marks of…Love?	1
2	I Will Give You Rest	5
3	An Empty House	9
4	God in the Kitchen Sink	12
5	Waiting in the Darkness	15
6	Feed Me	18
7	Just a Touch	22
8	What If It Hurts?	26
9	Blowing Wishes	29
10	You Can't Buy It	32
11	A Perfect Disaster	35
12	Demanding Your Love	41
13	Let Me Out of Here	44
14	Watch Me!	47

MAMA PRAYS

15	Potty Training	49
16	The You Beneath the Screams	52
17	For Everyone but Me	56
18	Just Visit	59
19	Let It Be	61
20	It's Scarier in the Dark	64
21	Talitha Koum	67
22	Wailing for Waffles	69
23	Multiply Me	73
24	Motherhood, or Why I'm Still in My Pajamas	76
25	Love in a Pile of Shoes	79
26	This is My Body	81
27	Come out of Your Hiding Place	85
28	Look into the Face of Love	87
29	Stay with Me	89
30	Via Dolorosa	91
	About the Author	94

ACKNOWLEDGMENTS

This book would not exist without the support of my husband Garrett or the inspiration of my children. Your love is my life and the fuel that keeps me going. Many thanks are due to Caitlan Rangel, my dear friend, constant cheerleader, and partner in the trenches of motherhood. Thanks also to Judy Stone, Johanna Dombo, Shirley Ireton, Laura Stribling, Sam Povlock, Shannon Evans, Bond Strong, Josh Beckman, Kendra Tierney, David Romero, and Christopher Kaczor, without whose support this book would never have taken shape, and to Catherine Sullivan for edits and feedback. And thank you to my parents, who introduced me to Jesus, put me through over a decade of Catholic school, and didn't bat an eye when I "threw it all away" to be home with my children – which is where my writing and these prayerful reflections on motherhood really began.

1 MARKS OF...LOVE?

I didn't love the way I looked in a bikini before I had children. I fretted over perceived imperfections, poured time and money into fixing them. I drank green juices, combined cardio with weights, and observed the scale intently for feedback about my efforts. I gave up sugar. I worked out daily, often twice a day. I sacrificed the joy of cooking hearty, delicious meals because comfort food doesn't lead to a smaller waistline. And, as it always is with the paradox of perfectionism, the more "success" I had, the more consumed with my flaws I became. It was how they say it is with drugs; the little wins were no longer "high" enough; I needed "more" to feel the same level of satisfaction. More pounds lost, more compliments, more heads glancing my way as I passed.

Here I am, two weeks postpartum, afraid to look in the mirror. Tiny streaks scream red across a crinkling mass of skin. Nine months of stretching taught and full, it now hangs loose. Like a discarded dress crumpled on the floor, there's no body now to give it form. Pangs of regret and shame well up and spill over, tears hot and angry on my cheeks. Shame compounds shame as I berate myself for these feelings over what is superficial, what should be trivial. As my stomach slowly shrinks after baby number two, I remember how I looked in a bikini before having children, and I feel so many things about myself - all of them ugly.

Derision towards my past self for having so little appreciation for my own beauty before it was stolen. Resentment of my pregnant self for doing so little to prevent this. Impatience with my current self for feeling these, for feeling so much regret over something that is both beyond my control and reflects nothing of my character. Sadness for my husband, who has more love in his life than ever, but at the cost of a less beautiful wife. More than any of it, I want to be beautiful for him again.

"Unless a grain of wheat falls to the ground and dies, it can bear no fruit," (Jn 12:24).

In order for something greater to grow, something lesser has to die.

My stomach stretches taut again, home to another growing baby. I pass myself in the mirror and this time, I allow myself to really look. I see the red lines, faded now to purple. They are less noticeable, but assuredly permanent. The more dramatic difference is internal. I see the evidence of beauty marred, what was lost that I once wept so bitterly for and recognize that just as time has faded these marks, it has also transformed my feelings.

As dearly as it's cost me, I'd rather be left with these stretch marks than my vanity. Each line is a chain broken, a door to deeper freedom, a chance to let go. I was, as St. Paul says, a slave to things of this world, and in many ways I still am. But my stretch marks are a reminder of Who and what I am living for. I am made for the dynamism of eternity, not the static stillness of a fashion magazine. Did I know this before? Of course. But it is one thing to know a thing. To live a truth is something else entirely.

The more painful crucible has been learning to let my husband love me - me, as I am. The longer we are married, the more the illusion that I can earn his love is shattered. My gifts of cookies and kisses and lipstick used to go to him with a price tag, an expectation of affection offered in return. The smaller, the weaker, the lesser I am, the more deeply I understand the power and the purity of his love. The way to receive a gift is to accept it, not to try to pay for it. I married him willing to accept something so much cheaper than what he was prepared to give me. The marks on my body don't reflect the state of my soul, but somehow, they have helped me to see and surrender my own woundedness more clearly. They free me just a little bit more from the burden of having to prove my own loveliness. They are a gift - the marks of the love we have born, and the opening to a well of love that runs even deeper still.

2 I WILL GIVE YOU REST

There will be no nap today.

The realization hangs heavy around my chest as I watch my plans evaporate. Some days, I'm ready to embrace the opportunity. Conscious of how quickly each stage of babyhood passes, I'm content simply to gaze at the little one folded into my arms. I watch as parted lips draw breath through a tiny "o." It's a quiet exchange only God could have dreamed up - the peace my children find in my arms, and the love that swells for them as we rest together in the stillness. But today, ugliness breaks through and instead of soaking in motherly affection, all I can access is bitter frustration. I know the invitation in this moment is to lay down my attachment to the to-do list, to stop clothing myself with accomplishments to prove I am worthy - even when those accomplishments are as meager as taking out the trash and sweeping the floor.

MAMA PRAYS

It's a lesson I'm hard-pressed to learn, apparently, because God keeps giving me fitful sleepers. I've read every book there is on sleep, but after birthing two babies on opposite ends of the personality spectrum, all I can do is throw my hands up in the air and add naps to the list of life's unfathomable mysteries. I think I'll pencil it in right below the Trinity.

You are busy with many things.

Exactly, Lord, so why don't you dispatch a saint or two to sing this kid to sleep?

Come to me, you who are labored and burdened, and I will give you rest.

Rest. Right. "Sleep when the baby sleeps." Whoever came up with that sound advice had only one kid and a housekeeper.

Choose the better part.

What is "the better part" here? How is resting possibly going to help? Everything that needs doing will still be waiting, and I'll have a baby to nurse and a toddler to entertain when we get there.

But who will you be when you get there?

And it clicks. Through a fog of sleeplessness, memories of my Ignatian training emerge. The phrase "cura personalis" comes into focus, and I begin to see all the ways I haven't been practicing "care of the whole person." The heavy shackles of my to-do list include the tasks necessary to care for everyone else. My own needs appear nowhere, as though I am a Superhero – or maybe just nonexistent. Things like "read a book," "call a friend," "have a cup of tea," "take a shower" - these don't make it onto the list. These, the lie goes, are selfish luxuries, privileges I let go of when I chose to be a mom.

You cannot serve from an empty vessel.

Oops.

Why do I so often forget that taking care of others requires that I be healthy and whole? Dancing to my favorite music, enjoying a hot cup of coffee, going for a run - these are gifts God has given me to recharge. Saying "no" to these is refusing to accept the graciousness of God. When I withhold the little things that bring me joy until I've completed my "daily requirements" list, I enslave myself to the "to-do" list. Taking time to relish the little joys of life is accepting the gift that is this world. It is taking God's outstretched hand and bringing him into my day. It's not that the list of things to do shrinks while I am otherwise engaged but taking the time to nourish my soul at the banquet of gratitude

MAMA PRAYS

means that when I do return to my tasks, I give out of fullness. Rather than labor as a starving slave, I am filled with the goodness of God, ready to overflow this graciousness as I go about my day.

God, like a mother putting her child to bed, wants to give me rest. I glance at my now soundly sleeping baby. Who am I to refuse?

3 AN EMPTY HOUSE

I love the quiet, the stillness before the sun rises and little feet patter down the hall. This time is my gift to myself and to God. It is the time when the coffee is still hot, and my soul is more contemplative than chaotic. This time is a treasure, bought with reluctant obedience to an early alarm. Having traded sleep for silence, I feel so deprived when unexpected needs arise. I meet the cries and sleepy hugs of early risers with the covetous heart of a child whose candy has just been snatched away.

And yet, on a morning like this, when the beds are void of kids who've spent the night at their grandmother's, the emptiness of the house becomes vacant space in my soul. I look forward so wistfully to my stolen moments alone, time to catch my breath and regain lost ground on projects lying fallow for want of attention. But in this moment, the silence is not the voice of solitude, but a prophetic anticipation of the quiet that looms inevitably ahead.

One day, the counters won't be sticky, and the floor will be free of crumbs. The washer won't rewash so many loads gone undried. Beds will stay made.

My writing time will be free of interruptions.

These thoughts should liberate me, the finish line at the end of a breathless race. Beyond that finish line awaits its own kind of beauty. But nothing, these moments remind me, worth skipping ahead to greet.

As G.K. Chesterton is rumored to have said, 'The way to love anything is to realize that it may be lost." My little shooting stars will be here so brief a time, and their littleness gone even quicker still.

One day, this empty house will be filled with the echoes of songs sung, pages turning, towers crashing, and squeals of delight. It will resonate with the sounds of memories made, not haunted by moments wasted. The house will be empty, and my heart will ache, but I will be wanting for the goodness that was rather than wishing for what could have been.

When I'm left in the stillness with writing as my solace, how grateful I will be for the moments it

MAMA PRAYS

was writing that I set aside for my children, and not the other way around.

4 GOD IN THE KITCHEN SINK

This house will never be clean again.

Despite the unlikelihood of this statement, I know it to be true. I'm drowning in a sea of toys and laundry, and if I am to take Marie Kondo's advice, it's all going in the trash because none of it is sparking any joy.

The kitchen is my one respite. Even on the most hectic of days, the kitchen remains the place where I can still check off the boxes. Meals will be prepared and served. The dishwasher will be loaded, and the coffee set for tomorrow. This room is proof of my productivity, and for that, I love it.

St. Teresa of Calcutta must have loved it, too, or else why would she offer this advice to her sisters: "Wash the dish not because it is dirty, nor because you are told to wash it, but because you love the person who will use it next." My Confirmation saint, St. Teresa of Avila offered this consoling advice: "Know that when you are in the kitchen, our Lord moves amongst the pots and pans." The kitchen, then, must be some sort of blissful haven for many of us overwhelmed by the endless cycle of domestic responsibilities, right?

Well, maybe not. Maybe these Teresas, these powerhouses of virtue, had access to dispositions honed by years of practice. Not one that sought to deny the value of the work of their vocations, but to sanctify each task in the offering of a joyful, obedient soul.

I am not a Teresa.

My invitation to holiness is at the kitchen sink, where I enjoy the steady, soapy warmth of the water washing plates clean again. It's in the oven and at the stove, where favorite scents marry. It is on the dinner table where I offer my family nourishment, the Eucharist of our domestic church and the foreshadowing of the heavenly banquet to come. In these places, grace and gratitude flow naturally, tied to these little acts of service that I love as a mother.

Past the kitchen, through the garage door, lurks my nemesis: a pair of dark and humid machines whirling endlessly, the rhythmic tapping of jean zippers on metal a constant reminder that there is more to be done. I fold stubborn fabric that has passive-aggressively gathered itself into a thousand wrinkles, tossing the unwearable pieces straight back into a hamper that mocks me with its ability to remain obstinately full. I glance at the painting of the Polish Madonna hanging sheets on the line, and this image reminds me that here, too, is where I meet God.

Every folded shirt and orphaned sock neatly stored is an occasion for holiness. When I greet these tasks with prayer and purpose, I say "goodbye" to the gloom in my soul. I allow God's warmth to penetrate me until I radiate his own goodness. That is the path of virtue. That is what it means to be a saint. I am all that stands between me and this quiet loveliness. So, I will go now to greet the laundry basket with a smile, with gratitude for its heft. The weight of these many baskets full means that there are loved ones to clothe, and abundance that clothes them. I will fold and stash each garment with love in my fingers, imagining the caress of this fabric as an extension of my own embrace. I would rather be weeding in the garden, standing at the sink, or snuggling with my little ones. I would rather so many other things. But this is the work of the moment. This is the task at hand.

And so, I surrender. I trust God to iron all out my little wrinkles, starting here, in this laundry basket, with a joyful "yes."

5 WAITING IN THE DARKNESS

We are scheduled for an 11 pm induction.

The house is dark and quiet, and somehow feels hollower with my daughter sleeping at her grandmother's instead of her little bed. My belly aches with weight as I shift positions on the couch. The baby stretches, too, and a tiny ripple runs through the skin stretched taught. This will be my last night feeling him inside of me.

I didn't want to be induced. This wasn't my choice. I had spent months reading about and preparing for a natural birth, gathering electric tealights and lavender oil, my birth ball and playlist of calming music. I wanted to be fully present to this experience of motherhood, to avoid the epidural, to move through labor, to avoid even the slightest possibility of a C-section, especially dangerous for my high-risk blood-clotting condition. I had my own plans, but the doctor thought otherwise. After two weeks of prodromal labor, labor that progressed in fits and spurts, putting us on edge to dash to the hospital at any moment, like runners filled with tension at the start, ready to spring into the race at any moment. We were already fatigued from the intention of holding this constant readiness. I had my own plans, but as the doctor informed us, it was time to get this baby out.

Lord, take this cup from me, I pray. I ache to birth this baby without Pitocin, without the unbearable pain I'd heard medicinally strengthened contractions could bring. Doubt swirls in my chest. My husband's nickname for me is" "delicate flower." I believe my body was created to give birth, but I think little of my own ability to withstand the extra intensity of medically induced contractions.

Not as I will, but as you will, I surrender.

Outside of Holy Thursday Mass, I adore Jesus who looks at me out of a small, white circle. I lost my family in the procession, this mass of people seeking to be close to him. We huddle together under a white tent, large, but not large enough to contain us, with only candlelight and song to fill the darkness of the night around us. It is several months later, my son safely birthed and sleeping soundly at home. My chest dampens by way of reminder as full breasts leak through the fabric of my dress. *I should go home,* I think. Home to my husband and my children who slumber silently on.

I can't pull myself away. I want to sit with Jesus in the darkness, in the anticipation of his pain. It brings to the surface memories of my own dark night of waiting, of willingly submitting to the pain that brings new life. I remember the intensity of the contractions, the relief of my husband's mere touch, the searing burn of pain as my son emerged, and the utter joy and awe as they placed love upon my chest.

In this moment too, this Holy Thursday passion, we know the joy that comes at the end of the darkness. The victory is sure. Still, we sit with Jesus as he prays. We keep watch as he anticipates. We suffer alongside his suffering. We bring our suffering to the God who suffers with us, who knows too well the sting of injustice and loneliness, the poverty of rejection and revulsion. We all have our moments of darkness and sometimes, as in the birth of my son, it is easy to see the dawn of Easter on the horizon. During others, the night seems longer. The darkness is blacker. Dawn seems an impossibility. On those nights, we light candles and keep watch with Jesus in the garden. And as we wait for the dawn, we take comfort in the stars, the tiny signs that darkness never fully reigns. Even from untravellable distances, light touches us, breaks up the darkness, and reminds us to hope.

6 FEED ME

Can a baby be addicted to nursing?

I wonder. My daughter, my first child, is a few weeks old and gaining weight steadily. And it's no wonder: she eats, she sleeps, and she cries. Nursing is our precious time, our time when she is content and quiet. It is a relief from her otherwise relentless cries. In the hospital, she latched on and didn't stop. I wondered, *could she be that hungry?* After 45 minutes, the nurse came in and showed me how to release the latch, assuring me my newborn had gotten enough.

My little girl, it turned out, didn't have an "enough" when it came to nursing. For months, our sessions closed with me removing her or, more often, with her drifting into unconsciousness. But her need for me didn't stop there.

MAMA PRAYS

...

It's six months later, and my fingers tap way on a keyboard next to her sleeping head on the queen-sized mattress in her nursery. Leaving her to nap alone is not an option. A first-time mom, I am tense with anxiety about her rolling off the bed, suffocating from SIDS, and above all, her supernatural ability to sense the proximity of my body and wake in fitful tears upon finding my absence. It is less stressful to bring my laptop into the room, to work as she rests next to me on the bed, and gaze wistfully at the crib I had ignorantly painted in blissful joy just months earlier. I wonder if it will ever cradle a sleeping bed, or if it will permanently become the decoration it now serves as. I had known that she would be born helpless. I hadn't anticipated her need, her attachment, her hunger not only for my milk but for my arms, my touch, my nearness.

...

"Mommy, will you lay with me?" It is three years later, and she finally sleeps alone, in her own bed, crib outgrown. She has long since stopped nursing, but her need for my touch continues with surprising intensity. She wants my hands to hold hers as we walk, my lap to perch on as we read, my kiss to cover her pain. My nearness is comfort, and I suppose now I understand. What could be more powerful than being enveloped by love?

MAMA PRAYS

...

I am pregnant with another son, bump bruised and tender from daily injections that reduce my risk of blood clots. A mess of arms of legs scramble over me on the couch, more interested in coming close to me than whatever cartoon flickers across the TV screen. As they clamor for cuddles, vying for a seat in my quickly disappearing lap, the bruises on my belly sting in protest. I wince, but my arms envelop my snugglers anyway.

...

My body is not my own. It can be frustrating and overwhelming, this call to give when I'm exhausted, to open my arms and my lap when I'd rather lay down. I stoop to pick up and carry kids with outstretched arms, kids who can walk but reach out to me anyway, "Up!" Although they've learned to balance, they are still learning that they're loved. Aren't we all?

Motherhood is a call to be touched. Our bodies are a living sacrifice. Little hands and little hearts depend on us. Long after our milk runs dry, our bodies mysteriously continue to feed our hungry children. "This is my body, given for you," we say, and even before they are old enough to receive the Eucharist, they know what it means to consume our love.

MAMA PRAYS

Yes, it is exhausting, and its physicality is overwhelming. But the physical sacramentally points to a deeper reality. Our is a call to be not depleted, but to give out of our poverty like the widow who gave her last coins. This means giving our bodies again and again. It means giving our love, patience, and attention, even when the inner bank seems empty. Sometimes, we choose to put more stock in our own emptiness than in serving these little ones in need. But more often, we experience the miracle and mystery that is love: in being poured out, it only grows. Like the flour of Elijah's widow, or the oil that burned in the temple for the Maccabees, love is actually inexhaustible.

And what is a mystery to me is plainly clear to my children: love is in these hands, and that is why they reach out again and again to grab them.

7 JUST A TOUCH

My daughter's body is curled on my chest, hot with fever. She is 18 months old, just discovering the joy of running everywhere, but this week her little legs lay still. She opens her eyes some, vaguely aware that Dory is getting lost for the 18th time on the blue of the television screen. The dishes stay in the sink, the laundry goes unfolded, and someone else carries out my lesson plans at work. My most important job needs doing, and I wouldn't trade it for anything.

If I but touch his clothes, I will be healed.

My young children seem to have the same insight as the woman with the hemorrhage: physical contact heals. When they are sick, just being in my arms is a form of treatment. There is Tylenol, nasal spray, popsicles, lots of rest, and being held by mom. This

is my natural superpower: in making me their
mother, Christ made me the hem of his garment, a
conduit of comfort and pain-relieving grace. It is
not much, to be held, but when you are suffering,
when you don't understand why or whether it will
end, trusting the strength and assurance of the arms
holding you might be all there is.

And so, I hold my daughter close. I let her sleep,
cry, and press against me. Time stops at our house
this week. My world narrows only to her. I know
this week will end, but she doesn't. This week, she
gets all of me. More than the medicine, she needs
me. My body next to her brings peace, healing the
disquiet in her soul.

Years later, we have that same couch, and we still
snuggle on it. She's too big now to fit on my chest.
Now, she lays close beside me. I don't remember
what was in those lesson plans I missed teaching
that week. Likely, neither do those students who
were there during my absence. Years ago, a youth
leader of mine encouraged us to learn to distinguish
in our lives between what is *urgent* and what is
important. Often, he said, we neglect the non-urgent
important things because the urgent things are
pressing. They demand our attention and must be
done in a timely way. But, he said, that time we
neglect the important for the urgent adds up.
Sometimes, we have to set aside what is merely
urgent for what is truly important.

MAMA PRAYS

Jesus was on his way to heal a little girl that day in the crowd when the woman with the hemorrhage reached out to him for healing. And the touch of his garment did heal her. She got what she needed. Jesus could have just passed her by and continued on his way. He didn't. He chose to stop and speak to this woman face to face. This woman who, for twelve years, had been ritually impure because of her illness and excluded from Temple worship. A little girl lays dying, but Jesus stops. He doesn't let this woman go unnoticed. His touch has healed her, and still, he takes the time to be present with her.

Were my students also important that week? Of course they were. And someone well-qualified was there, taking care of their needs. Who is qualified to mother our children in our absence? My daughter needed me that week. Me. My arms to hold her, my fingers to stroke the hair off her forehead, my voice singing her to sleep. The gift of presence is mysterious. As much as my daughter needed me that week, she will likely never remember that childhood illness. She won't remember, but I will never forget.

Now that I'm home with them full time, do I still have that kind of clarity? How many times do piles of dishes and loads of laundry seem more urgent and pressing than my children's requests to play Candyland? It can be a challenge, choosing the important in the midst of urgent messes. And I can't neglect the things that need doing in our home every time. The challenge is doing them without forgetting that right now, my most important ministry is to let them crawl up on my lap and read a book.

8 WHAT IF IT HURTS?

My daughter's skin is all patches of pink. It cracks from dryness, little rivers of red flowing where her fingernails have etched tiny scratches. I feel the pain of her eczema in my own body. I ache to offer her some relief, to apply the salve I know will lessen her discomfort. She cowers behind the toilet in tears, terrified of my touch. To her, it doesn't mean healing. It's the unknown. These creams have burned and itched in the past; she isn't going to trust me now.

Another night, same struggle. This time I don't blame her for her fear; I'd be afraid, too, if someone twice my size walked towards me with a knife. She's taken creative liberty with the floss she brought home from the dentist's office, and now it's wrapped too tightly around her neck. "This won't hurt," I promise, beckoning her to come to me. She won't come of her own will. Even after I've cut her free, she's still screaming, "I'm not ready!" her fear wrapped around her so tightly she doesn't realize she's not bound anymore.

She reacts like this every time: to the tweezers when she stuffed a ball up her nose, the antibiotics we had to administer as eye drops, the syringe filled with grape-tinged fluid. All our attempts at healing, whether to ameliorate illness or save her from herself, are met with fear.

Why? I ask. Have I ever been anything but good to her? Why doesn't she trust me?

Probably for the same reasons I don't trust God, I think.

It's easy to trust God in a general sort of way. I love verses like Jeremiah 29:11: "For surely I know the plans I have for you, says the Lord, plans for your welfare and not for harm, to give you a future full of hope." I believe in his ultimate plan for my good.

I'm also afraid it might hurt.

What if he asks me to do something difficult? What if his call is to carry a cross I don't want to bear? The further along I travel in this vocation of motherhood, the more deeply I realize the potential for human pain that comes with loving this way, that loss might truly break me. I hesitate to approach God even for the simplest and most profound form of spiritual healing in the Sacrament of Reconciliation, because, like antiseptic on a wound, it burns a little bit.

But then, God did not make me to live in fear.

As St. Paul writes, "God did not give us a spirit of cowardice but rather of power and love and self-control," (2 Tim 1:7). My daughter's fear and littleness will not last forever. Nor should mine. Fortitude is a gift of the Spirit, as well as cardinal virtue. The Christian life is a call to courage. As Pope Benedict XVI said, "The world promises you comfort, but you were not made for comfort. You were made for greatness." Yes, the healing God offers might smart a bit. His plan for my salvation might mean walking a road I wouldn't choose myself. But even Jesus drank a cup he would rather have left untouched. In the end, trusting our Father is an exercise without condition. We submit ourselves to a love that has greater plans for us than mere protection. He allows us to walk in our pain, but he doesn't waste it.

I hope one day my daughter learns to trade her fear for trust.

I hope that I do, too.

9 BLOWING WISHES

My toddler loves dandelions. He wanders to them, one after the next, gathering their wispy heads close to his lips. Sometimes the seeds stick to his wet lips as he tries to scatter them with his breath, to blow and spread their wild beauty on the breeze. He delights in this simple act: gather and spread, gather and spread.

The ancient philosophers, too, recognized something of what it is that allows for such simple pleasures. It is the wonder of being, the amazement that there is anything at all when there could just be nothing. The world *is*, and that fact alone gives rise to awe.

It takes time for children to develop qualities like strength of character and virtue, or the knowledge of when to yell and when to be quiet. The ability to finish a plate of peas. But children never have to be told to wonder at the world. That is innate, something that we lose as we grow, if we're not careful. The ability to wonder at bubbles as they float past and pop, to giggle as squirrels chase each other through trees, this is a gift our unhurried children have in spades. This is the same gift that fuels the joy children take in running at full speed across a field and scaling the tallest of jungle gyms just to slide back down again and again and again. They know that the world is good, and they know how to revel in it.

Dandelion seeds blow by and float away. They settle unseen and take root. They must, because no matter how frequently my son picks all the flowers in sight, new ones pop up to take their place. Their bright yellow faces turn gray and frail, ready to fall apart at the slightest touch. Yet this delicate nature is not a weakness; it is precisely this falling apart to be blown on the wind that leads to so many more flowers in a field. Because this bloom gives it life, many more will grow. I see the beauty in the scattering of seeds, a metaphor for the central spiritual truth of the cross. I can analyze, contemplate, and ponder. For all of my thoughts, none propels me forward to snap a stem and blow wishes on the breeze.

My son needs none of this reflection. The sight of the dandelion alone is enough. It's existence signals the possibility to participate in and enjoy the goodness of God's creation. The fact that it *is* is enough for him to respond.

How many chances do I miss in this life because I pause to wonder whether they are worth taking? I analyze rather than assume the goodness of the world. I calculate cost and benefit. Rarely do I see the unknown through hopeful eyes that anticipate opportunity. More often, I am a little anxious about preventing all that could possibly go wrong. This is an important mark of adulthood, being able to think ahead and plan wisely. But when worry eclipses our enjoyment of life, a treasure has been lost. When Jesus invites us to consider the birds and the lilies, how God meets their needs through no effort of their own, he might also be inviting us to consider our children. They laugh, they trust, they revel in the goodness of the world. I know too much of the world to live a carefree life but growing up doesn't have to mean the death of wonder. Wonder is innate, but it can be lost for lack of use. And so, I lean forward. I take hold of the stem. I bring the flower to my lips, and blow.

10 YOU CAN'T BUY IT

My first birth tore me open. For a month, I could barely shift positions, let alone walk and care competently for our colicky newborn. I was still taking heavy painkillers to dull the pain, and the weight of failure hung around me. My daughter wouldn't stop crying and my body was so broken that I could barely hold and walk her through it. That wasn't the worst part though.

Everything about motherhood was new. I hadn't expected that it would be this hard, but I also hadn't really known what to expect. What cut me more was the struggle I had accepting help from my husband. I didn't want him to care for me. I didn't want to ask for that glass of water or help up off the couch. I didn't want him making us meals. That was my territory. Cooking, homemaking, caretaking - these were my specialties, my contribution to our marriage. Now that the birth of our daughter had left me unable to accomplish them, even temporarily, I floundered.

He was working so hard to take care of us. He would work all day to earn a living, and then come home to a sobbing wife holding a fussy baby and offer me some relief from the physical pain and emotional pressure I put on myself. These days were hard, but they were made harder by the fact that I couldn't accept his hard work and kind gestures as love. Instead, they were proof of my own inadequacy.

I've always struggled with the drive to cheapen love into currency. Accepting the mystery of love's gratuitousness has not come easily. I don't want gifts. I would rather earn my way into affection. It is steadier ground to stand on something you deserve. This is a false security fed by the lie that I can weave my deserving web all the time. It is shaky ground, trusting someone else with your heart. People fail. They are inconsistent. They are trapped by their shortcomings, history, and failures. But the shaky ground of love freely given is still more real than the illusion that I can garner, hold, and deserve love by my own will.

My husband doesn't dole out love because I am worthy. He loves me because *he* is good. The more unable I am to perform, the more I free I am to enter into the divine mystery of love. This Sacrament shines light on the truth of God's love; it is not dependent on me. I so want to stay in the safety of performing and earning affection. It is more familiar. It fills me with pride. But it is also much more like slavery than love. Ironically, the less I am able to do, the freer I am. When I accept and embrace love freely given despite my limitations, the shackles fall off. The less I have to say about *why* my husband or God loves me, the more fully their love fills me. Love and grace flowing freely from a giver of good gifts. The more that is stripped away, the more easily I recognize this truth. The more easily I receive it.

That's nice, isn't it?

Sure it is. And yet I still find myself praying alongside a young St. Augustine, more scoundrel than saint: *Yes, Lord, I want this gift.*

Just - not yet.

MAMA PRAYS

11 A PERFECT DISASTER

It's December 27th and the house is as quiet as the snow that silently blankets everything outside of our windows in the predawn blackness.

The only light in the room glows from our Christmas village where it sits merrily on the mantle, high above greedy fingers whose enthusiasm threatens to crack its delightfully delicate rendition of an idyllic Christmas. The sight the villagers look down upon, however, is another story.

Our family's living room speaks of a Christmas that is far from idyllic. The tree skirt is rumpled, and one tiny Santa ornament has attempted escape, managing to settle limply where he has rolled mere feet away. A single stocking has fallen, and lays defeated, empty and crumpled at the foot of the fireplace. The lower half of the tree, once glittering in festive Christmas glory, is now bare save the lights that peek out between its branches. The tree's top half remains ornamented like the tip of a mountain whose snow line creeps down only so far, except the tree line is one that ascends rather than descends – exactly the height of tiny fingers whose curiosity cannot be contained, whose fascination drives them to pluck each ornament for examination and redistribution across the house. Like a squirrel storing up nuts for the snowy season, my 18-month-old has tucked away ornaments in every corner of the house, storing up surprises in case toys run scarce. I imagine we will still be discovering them amongst the Easter eggs in April.

If God has graced your home with the unabashed joy of little ones this season, then I suspect yours, too, is a bit more disheveled than the average yuletide greeting card. Perhaps your dustpan and superglue are expecting time and half for the extra hours put in scraping up and mending glittery remnants that trail in your toddler's wake. Perhaps, like ours, your Christmas Mass felt fragmented, the elegant liturgy and deeply prayerful homily shattered in your mind by sibling squabbles and discovery of the too-noisy toys your children have smuggled in by their tapping against the pews. Maybe, instead of a delectably and artfully frosted sugar cookie, your bits of prayer were really more like the crumbs that Santa left behind. Maybe the joy of this feast feels distant, observed, and untasted.

If you had a Christmas like mine in which the wreckage threatens to eclipse and the tantrums to drown out the gift of this season, I invite you to once again consider that first Christmas evening – preferably in quiet solitude while sipping on a heated beverage of your choosing. Consider Joseph's first Christmas. Joseph must have arrived in Bethlehem feeling like an utter failure. Who hauls a woman across the countryside at nine months pregnant? Joseph's insignificance left him powerless against the governmental forces requiring their travel. What kind of husband can't secure shelter for his laboring wife? Joseph's meager living meant he had nothing to bargain with. What kind of father allows his son to be born amidst the stench of manure?

What kind of God entrusts a man like this to shelter and protect the birth of Salvation?

Joseph's first Christmas was a perfect disaster.

I sympathize with Joseph. My 18-month-old – the ornament snatcher – was born in May of 2020 at the height of the pandemic. Despite our family having no illness, no symptoms of illness, my husband was barred from the delivery room and my son was taken away from me immediately after birth. My husband did everything he could, rushing our older children to their appointed caretakers and arriving in time to stand knocking at the door while I labored alone just beyond. My delivery room may have been a bit more sanitary than Mary's stable floor, but the situation wreaked of similar indifference and injustice. Having been told by his wife that all she needed to get through her high-risk birth was his hand to hold, my husband was wracked with fury at his powerlessness to provide even that.

This is how I imagine Joseph arriving at the first Christmas: exhausted from a grueling journey, anxious about his wife's safety, guilty and humiliated about her lack of comfort, furious at the lack of hospitality and compassion, and entirely ashamed of his failure to provide. All of the stench and the dirt and the frustration was the reality of that first Christmas.

And yet.

And yet none of it could eclipse the brightness of the greatest miracle of human history up through that point. God made flesh. Salvation, incarnate. The Lord of Lords and the Prince of Peace chose to descend to us in the midst of the dirt and the manure. He chose Joseph with all of his apparent inadequacies as the protector of His mother. And He selected the poor and dirty shepherds as His first visitors – not the gold-bearing Wise Men. Jesus is revealed to us first as poor, and then as king.

How easy it is for us to believe that only the shiny gifts are good. In all of the dust and the shame and the deep inconvenience of that first Christmas, Mary and Joseph didn't miss the miracle. The real Christmas, be it that very first night or the daily dawning of Christ in our hearts, is rarely ever shiny. Love is messy. It happens in the muck between imperfect people who wound each other and look past the mess to the miracle that we have one another at all. Christ doesn't choose to arrive in perfect circumstances. He never did.

There was a time in our marriage when every strand of tinsel stayed where I placed it. No ornaments cracked, my chosen guests devoured my meticulously prepared delectations that no one ever declared "icky," and at Mass I prayed in blissful peace through every chorus of "Oh Come All Ye Faithful." It was clean, orderly, and entirely pleasing.

Of course, the God who subverts all our expectations gives us gifts wrapped not in crisp paper and bright bows, but in sticky jam hands and tiny faces streaked with tears shed over disasters both real and imagined. He delights more in the toddler with her head in the pew and her ankles in the air bellowing "Away in the Manger" than in the stiffness of the most perfect posture at the kneelers. After all, it is He who gave us children, who made them to wonder with wide eyes and explore with insatiable curiosity this world that He has given us. It was Christ who beckoned the children to himself, knowing full well that they are children, and that his dusty robes would become even dustier and stickier by their embrace.

Family life is hard. It is messy and exasperating and often reaches the decibels of a jet engine at takeoff. And it is a miracle of endless significance, as each new soul we welcome stretches into eternity. All the broken ornaments and backtalk in the world can't erase the magnitude of Christ's love for a single one of us. God wraps his most beautiful gifts in mud and in muck and the real, and we have to get messy if we want to receive them.

My greatest gift this Christmas season? Sitting here in the darkness, reveling in a rumpled tree skirt and half-decorated Christmas tree and knowing that this year, at least, I didn't miss the miracle.

MAMA PRAYS

12 DEMANDING YOUR LOVE

"Book!" says my toddler as he hobbles along, dragging a board book behind him. I take it from him and gather him onto what's left of my lap, shrinking away as the new baby grows within it. He smiles and bounces excitedly - his way of letting me know that I'm getting it right. This is how he gets my attention, by pressing himself into my hands. He insists.

In the morning, after naps, he cries out, "Mamma, out!" I pick him up. "Mamma, go!"

"Eat!"

"Outside!"

"Cuddle!" (My favorite)

MAMA PRAYS

The demands never cease. Nor does his confidence that I will respond. I am his mother, giver of good gifts. No need is too small. He voices them all, grabbing my finger and leading me when words fail him.

How often do I turn to God with this kind of confidence? I like to think that I do, but if I'm honest, more often the undertone of my requests in prayer is doubt, not trust. Not doubt that he hears me. Worse - doubt that he cares. I know I don't earn his love. God's affection and yeses in prayer are not dependent on the holiness of my soul. I know it in my head, but as a friend is fond of reminding me, the distance from our heads to our hearts is one of the longest to travel.

Yes, my prayers float like lilies on a pond: beautiful, blooming graces unfolding, floating in serenity. But doubt lurks just beneath the murky surface. Doubt that my little concerns matter. Doubt that I deserve him. Doubt that I really want His definition of "good" for me instead of my own. The pond beneath those lovely lilies is murky with mud.

The soul of a little child is, I think, more like a spring than a pond. Grace flows and does not stagnate. Sometimes only a trickle, but it is pure. This is what Jesus means, I think, when he asks us to become like little children. Not to whine, make messes that we refuse to clean up, or steal toys from our brothers; there is plenty of "rocky ground" for his grace to smooth away over time. To be like little children means to turn to him in all our need, to name those needs with expectation. We, even more than our children, have reason to expect his good gifts. Look at all he has given us. Despite his stellar track record, we still struggle to trust.

The secret that little children understand, the one that we forget, is that everything we have is a gift. It comes not by our own efforts, but at the grace of another. They don't hesitate to ask because they aren't trapped by the illusion that they have built their own good fortune. They, unlike us, know well their true littleness. And so, they don't hesitate to reach up their hands. They know that all good things come from above. Their witness teaches us to look up, reach out, and trust.

MAMA PRAYS

13 LET ME OUT OF HERE

"I hate you. I *hate* you!" my daughter screams from behind her door. Her words cut me, but this is hardly the first tantrum that we've weathered. I stand outside, deaf to the sound of kicks and screams. They used to break me inside; familiarity has numbed their sting.

"Let. Me. Out!" She punctuates every word with a pound of her fist against the door. This is her mantra, her fit of rage. I listen but I don't respond. In her anger, she has forgotten the truth: I am waiting for her outside. The door isn't locked. If she chose, she could walk back into my arms at any time. Instead, my prodigal daughter sits and stews in the fumes of her own fury.

This is where I vacillate as a parent. I waver between wanting to tow the hard line of justice and wanting to embrace her with arms of mercy. I want her to learn her lesson, to have the discipline to calm down and sort through her feelings and transgressions in a productive way. I want her to seek reconciliation. At the same time, I feel for her. I know the paralysis of the fear of rejection, even as an adult woman. I want to reach in, salve her pain, and help her breathe again.

On this day, when the screaming quiets, I walk through her door and scoop her up. Today, her hands do not push me away. Today, she crumples against me. The stiffness of fear and anger are gone. Her tiny hands clasp around my neck as she lets her head fall against my chest. When she is through soaking up affection and reassurance, she is ready to take my hand and walk out of her room. No, the door was never locked. Still, she needed a tangible sign to walk back through it.

This is the gift of confession, that tangible sign of the grace God offers us. We are never locked out. But, sometimes, we allow ourselves to be locked in by our own fears and shame. We let Satan twist us up on ourselves, sometimes so much that we blame God for the isolation we feel. We convince ourselves that it isn't even us who have done wrong. God is unfair and his rules are outdated. We ignore him. We pretend not to be hurt by consuming the things we know will consume us. We build our own prison walls, and then rail against God when we realize how trapped we've become.

There is an old tale of monkey-trapping in which a small piece of fruit is placed in a vessel with a long, small neck. The fruit is small enough to fit down there, but large enough that the opening becomes too tight for the fruit to be withdrawn once the monkey wraps his hand around it. There is nothing stopping the monkey from releasing the fruit and walking away. He remains trapped only as long as he refuses to let go of the fruit.

We imprison ourselves with our unwillingness to let go. We are trapped by the illusion of being trapped, locked in only because we are unwilling to try the handle and walk out of the darkness. Many times, freedom is not this easy, and our pain is not something we can simply walk away from.

But sometimes, it is.

MAMA PRAYS

14 WATCH ME!

"Watch me, Mommy!"

This is the single line of the chorus I hear all day long. Whatever task I am occupied by matters little to my daughter who burns to show me her latest accomplishment. From basketfuls of laundry and sinks full of dishes, I avert my gaze to behold new dances, record-breaking leaps, watercolor masterpieces, and puzzles completed. I wrestle with the need to finish what I'm doing and the desire to be present to her. And yet -

Every newborn yawn and scrunchy face was cause for awe. In the beginning, I didn't have to be reminded to watch; I could stare at her for hours. Every babble was precious. Where along the way did her existence become commonplace? How often do I miss what she is saying because her words are less important than whatever I am concentrating on?

"Watch me, Mommy!" This chorus is a grace. It is a reminder to give what I used to offer unbidden: my whole being attuned to this little, precious life. God has descended, etched his image on her soul, and asked *me* to care for her. Me. Does God issue a clearer call to love than the high-pitched wails of a newborn hungry for her mother's arms?

Of course, I am not called to keep my eyes on her unwaveringly. At the same time, I don't need a reminder to make dinner (just one to switch the laundry over!). This task to listen to little whispers and behold the unfolding of God's handwork in my children - this is the center of life and love. And still so often it seems that I relegate it to the whispering wind, God's voice so tiny that it doesn't resonate over the howling winds and raging fires of my life.

Thankfully, God in his wisdom has made children forgiving creatures. "Show me again," I say, and she is happy to comply.

15 POTTY TRAINING

Three days, they said on Pinterest, and even an 18-month-old could be using the toilet. A day and a half in and my two-and-a-half-year-old is no longer wearing diapers – she is using our whole house as a toilet. It's not really the mess that bothers me, although bending to wipe up and disinfect accidents at eight months pregnant poses its challenges. It's that preceding every accident or even successful use of the toilet, she gets nasty with me or erupts into a full-blown tantrum without warning.

I'm baffled. I'm frustrated. I'm tired. I'd expected messes, but I hadn't expected the emotional ones. She's sleeping in the backseat now. I glance at her still face in my rearview mirror. We're parked under the shade of the tree outside our large house, air-conditioning blasting. Normally naps are my time for rest as well, but today the thoughts are buzzing, and I cannot squash them quickly enough.

MAMA PRAYS

Is it too soon? Will she ever be able to do this? Am I able to do this? Am I a bad mother? I let them buzz. I'm too tired to answer. A leaf falls from the tree above and I stiffen as it hits the windshield. Did she hear it? Is she stirring? I'm not ready to let go of this moment of peace in our fitful days.

She shifts but her eyes remain closed, and I relax. I wonder - if I am so on edge, maybe this is stressful for her too. I look at her little body, completely sunk into the support of the car seat. Such relaxation in contrast to the stiffness that overtakes her in the bathroom. And then - clarity. She is anxious. The tantrums are portents of her fate to remain wild and untamed into adulthood. They're not a sign that we need to see a counselor immediately. They are her way of channeling feelings too big for her little body. She is worried and anxious about doing something she doesn't feel confident in her ability to do.

I can't imagine where she gets that from.

The realization brings such peace. I understand my mission now. This goes beyond teaching her to recognize physical signs and respond appropriately. This is the first of many lessons in how to respond when emotions overwhelm us. It dawns on my that up until now, parenting has involved a large learning curve, but it has basically been within my control. Keeping my cool during endless colic, being constantly on call for diaper changes and feeding sessions, picking up, carrying, buckling, washing, kissing booboos - all of it has been work, yes, but work in mastery of myself to respond to her needs. This is my first foray into cooperating with her to learn something. This is a moment to stop and pay attention.

What do I learn about my daughter from this process? She is, like her mother, easily frustrated by difficult tasks. She needs extra support and encouragement to learn something difficult. The unknown, when it demands that she perform, is overwhelming.

Up until now, her emotional needs have been simple and straightforward. No longer. Now, I begin the treacherous journey into something unknown, something difficult - something beyond what I feel prepared to accomplish. I know that she will learn to use a toilet eventually; there are few children who go to grade school lacking this ability. But will I be able to teach her resilience in the face of adversity? Can I equip her with better coping skills than I had as an anxious A-student, always dancing for love and applause, conflating the two? It's enough for panic to rise within me, and truthfully, I don't know. But I do know that I can always walk beside her and point her to the One who can.

MAMA PRAYS

16 THE YOU BENEATH THE SCREAMS

The heat is creeping towards 100 degrees today, so ice cream sounds like a good idea.

It could have been a good idea if my toddler had gotten her nap. Instead, we are out and about with my aunt, wandering up and down the blocks of quaint Old Town. She offers us this cool treat, and my daughter's eyes go big and round when she sees its size. Wired and full of sugar, we turn the corner to visit the next store, and my chest tightens. It's an old-fashioned toy store, displays of fun laid out at eye level, open and beckoning children to play and become attached. I steel myself for what lays ahead. This will not end well.

And it doesn't. All my "mom tricks" are insufficient to overcome the heat, exhaustion, and injustice my daughter feels at being exiled from toy utopia. The tantrum begins. All sweetness leaves her face, and a

MAMA PRAYS

tiny, contorted monster lets forth a shrill battle cry. I'm sure the toy store staff has seen their share of meltdowns, but the shame of failure grips my stomach. A better mother would have prevented this perfect storm of misery. I think of the car, several blocks away. I gauge the ability of my third trimester form to haul this screaming monster several blocks in this heat, calculate the approximate length of the tantrum, and I take a deep breath. Our only hope now is a swift exit.

I gather the flailing mass of limbs under my arm, ignoring the alarm of passersby as her wails of protest alert them to what may be a possible kidnapping. I silently thank God for our remarkable resemblance. Then again, I muse, a kidnapping persona might be preferable to that of a parent whose child can do *this*. I remember what I thought of parents who had kids like *these* before I became a mother. I didn't understand then that *all* kids are *this* kid some of the time.

I wrestle her into the car seat and drive the 20 minutes home. She is still screaming. I've blocked her out. What is she saying? Tuning back in, I register that she screams this phrase on repeat: "I WANT ANOTHER CHA-ANCE!" turning "chance" into a two-syllable word. "Cha-ance!" Me too, I think.

I want another chance to go back and insist that she gets her nap before we go out (or better yet, reschedule this outing for the morning). I want another chance to downgrade the size of her ice cream and to insist that we skip the toy store. I want another chance to go back and micromanage all the tiny details that led to this outburst. I sigh. Even if I had mitigated the tantrum by exerting every last ounce of control, we might still have ended up here, drowning in sweat and tears. There is one factor I *can't* control, the most important one. She is a toddler. The part of her that will regulate and control her behavior just isn't there yet. It isn't her fault. It isn't my fault. It's who we all are at some point.

What does loving her through this look like? How do I teach her that tantrums are unacceptable while also guiding her to own a sense of self-control? How do I exercise self-control when all the patience has drained from my body? These are the questions I wrestle with daily as I wonder if this phase will ever end.

As the shrieking slows to gasps and sobs, I quietly unbuckle her and take her into my arms. She shudders. Neither of us speaks. This was a hellish episode, perhaps the worst we've seen so far. I hold her until she grows heavier, and her body goes limp with sleep. I carry her into her bed and lay her down to rest. The sweetness has returned to her face. This episode is over.

I close the door quietly, tiptoe down the hall, and

sink into our couch as the realization overtakes me. Through these tantrums, my daughter is learning to exercise control. At the same time, my Father in heaven watches as I learn to surrender it.

MAMA PRAYS

17 FOR EVERYONE BUT ME

When I open the door and see my mother-in-law standing there, something inside cracks, and tears escape down my face. I'm not dressed. Toys and bits of food litter the floor. I've been wracked with piercing pain and illness for days. Merely dressing and feeding the children has been a feat; nothing about this environment speaks to my competency as a mother.

And yet, my tears are not of shame, but deep relief. I am so far past the breaking point, trapped inside my pain. This week has shattered any illusion that I can "do it all." I'd wanted to beg for help for days, but I stayed silent. It was my husband who finally called his mother to ask for help. Such a simple answer to everything I needed. I went in my room, closed the door, and slept for hours. My children were well cared for, the house spotless when I woke. Why hadn't I asked for help sooner?

A couple of years earlier, my daughter's babysitter fell ill during the Christmas break. A stay-at-home-mom, she didn't have childcare options on hand. Feeling the pain of caring for little ones during illness, I volunteered to take her girls for the day. It was blast - her girls are darlings, and my daughter was thrilled to have the extra playmates. It was so simple, the least I could do to show my gratitude for the love this woman poured out on my baby while I worked. Compassion and generosity compelled me to offer what little I could to ease her burden.

Why do I struggle so much to accept those same gifts? Why do I push away the generosity and compassion extended to me? It brings me such joy to be allowed to serve others in these ways, to give a little bit of my heart in kindness to someone else. What are these walls that trap me inside of myself when faced with my own needs?

These walls are dark, isolating, and ugly. They do not come from you, Lord. They keep out love and light, and trap me alone within. I've spent so much time cowering away from them, but now I want to know: what are they made of? I start to see them not as impenetrable boundaries, but for what they really are: unjust lies, impediments to love. And so, I investigate. I reach out my hand, expecting to feel cold stone. Instead, my hand passes through this barrier, and it disperses like wisps of smoke. There is nothing to this barrier that is substantial. My obedience to it is all that has locked me inside.

Habit keeps me inside these walls. If I press against these illusory stones, they fall. Knocking them aside will take time, but why not? All that waits on the other side is freedom and love. Lord, help me break down these walls, stone by stone.

Help is for everyone but me.

Love is for everyone but me.

Grace is for everyone but me.

One by one, they fall. The bits of these sentences that exclude me are lies that evaporate when exposed. Slowly, I am coming to accept that God's good gifts are for me, too. That others can and do love me, too. That his love is not only in the quiet moments, but in the concrete flesh and blood of his Body, of the missionaries of love that he has placed in my life. Help, love, and grace are for everyone. Period.

Thank you, Lord, that I am not that special.

18 JUST VISIT

I can't visit her. I'm taking care of two kids and I'm pregnant. *It's too far,* I brush the thought away, *and she probably wouldn't want the company anyway.*

But you did.

You traveled through your morning sickness to Elizabeth's side. Quickly. Did you visit because it was her time of need, or yours?

It's not the work I'm afraid of, or the burden of shuffling the kids back and forth. I prefer to think it's for ease, for the sake of my own comfort. Or even that my presence is somehow an unwanted intrusion, that staying away relieves her of the burden.

MAMA PRAYS

But really, I'm afraid.

I'm afraid I have nothing to give. I don't have any answers. I can't fix her pain or make her trials pass more quickly. I'm afraid to look at my own emptiness. After pouring myself into my children, my husband, our home - is there any "me" left to give? I'm more like a dried-out sponge than an empty vessel; I'll soak up whatever life there is to be had. And if I'm not there to give, what good am I then?

You were there "for" Elizabeth, but she gave as much to you. Despite her aching back and tired eyes, she reminded you of who are - blessed. In your youth and your fear, she affirmed you. Your visit was as much for you as it was for her.

This is our call. Not to give and give until there's nothing left. Not to define ourselves but what we can do, but to exchange ourselves, to share our souls with one another. We are to lift each other up, to be present to one another, to receive as much as we are to give. Motherhood is not something we do alone. We are not called to organize a meal train or buy the perfect shower gift; called to be *with* one another in our whole messy, broken reality.

MAMA PRAYS

19 LET IT BE

I laugh as the line turns pink. Earlier this week, I told my husband that although we had been trying to conceive our second child for a few months, just one week of juggling night school, full-time teaching, and taking care of our 2-year-old daughter had made me reconsider. I wanted to postpone through this last semester of graduate school. Now, I can only laugh as I unceremoniously hand the test to my husband. His laugh echoes mine as he places his hands on my belly. "Another baby," he whispers. We lock eyes and the reality of the life inside me takes hold. My narrow plans evaporate, love already blossoming.

Years later, a second line appears. And another, and another - all faint, but pink. I'm alone this time in a room empty of levity and laughter. I had successfully delivered our second child, a healthy boy, a year earlier after an anxiety-ridden pregnancy. A genetic condition exacerbated by pregnancy hormones had sent me to the ER coughing up blood, my lungs burning because of what we discovered was bilateral pulmonary embolisms - blood clots in both of my lungs. The shadow of a second line on this pregnancy test means something different to me now. New life, yes, but also grave danger to my own. I'm flooded with concerns for my husband as I anticipate his reaction, his anxiety more salient than my own. I run through his concerns, uncertain of how to ameliorate them: the blow to our finances, the added chaos to our relationship - still finding equilibrium with two under three – and most distressing of all, the possibility of losing me. There's nothing I can say. I sigh, eyes turned upwards, "Help?"

Grace descends, and with it, inexplicable peace settles as I tell my husband and see, to the astonishment of us both, that his response is one of joy. His response gives me permission to allow my own joy and relief to surface. Neither of us wanted to intentionally risk my life with another pregnancy. Both of us deeply desired to welcome another child.

My fears do not leave, resulting in anxious visits to the ER following imaginary but very real feeling burning in my lungs over the coming months. I understand that this pregnancy may demand my life. The pain of that thought, of leaving my husband and my little ones so soon, is enough itself to take my breath away. In these moments, I sit with my Mother, herself a young, unmarried girl whose pregnancy might cost her her life. She, too, knows that the joy of God's promise is great, and that nothing worthwhile comes without cost. We feel the shifts and jabs inside our expanding bellies and wonder about the person growing inside. Who will he grow up to be? We look at everything the Lord has done for us, the wild grace that has been our lives, and our hearts grow quiet. "Trust," she tells me, "Let it be."

20 IT'S SCARIER IN THE DARK

"Mommymommmymommy!" The breathless stringing together of my title is familiar, but the urgency with which my daughter calls is uncharacteristic. Her voice is laced with fear, so I rush into her room. The light of the early morning creeps into her room. It's not enough to eliminate the darkness, just enough to cast deep shadows.

In these shadows, apparently, lurks a monster. Cowering under her covers, my daughter points him out, and I wrestle him into the light. "See?" I pick him up and show her that the evil monster is actually a crumpled sweater, his mouth not full of jagged teeth, but an empty sleeve poking up from the pile of cloth below.

"That's not scary at all!" she exclaims.

MAMA PRAYS

Monsters, like most of life, are scarier in the dark. Sin and shame are most powerful when we let them whisper lies in our ears. We cover them up and turn off the lights so no one will see. What that really means is that we can't see them clearly either. In the dark, they lose their form, take on distorted shapes that trick and terrify us. We think we are safer in that darkened room, alone with these monsters. We don't want anyone else to see them. Terrifying as they are, we want to hide with them because, after all, we created these monsters. We deserve this fear. Shame traps us under the covers.

Freedom is as simple as crying out to our Father. He knows the landscape of our room. Our mess is not likely to trip him up. He is willing to enter our darkness, to pull us out of the beds we've made, and turn on the lights.

This is a different kind of scary. What we're likely to see is far less benign than a sweater; it is also often far less deadly than we imagine. The Father knows well the rooms of our hearts. It is not he who is afraid of facing our sin. We are. He wants to come in, to clean up, to take away the darkness and the pain and fear that rules when we face our sinfulness alone.

The thing about sin, though, is that it isn't just scarier in the dark. It's actually more dangerous. The darkness of sin doesn't lighten on its own; it's more like a black hole, absorbing the light, creating more and more darkness. And on our own, we can't resist its pull.

Luckily, we don't have to.

MAMA PRAYS

21 TALITHA KOUM

New life is waking up all around me. The first spring flowers yawn open. The bees pay a visit. A pink-headed hummingbird swoops down only to pause, suspended and in motion, so close I can see its feathers glisten. The green of seedlings planted weeks ago peek up from the blackness around them. All reminders of this simple fact: winter doesn't last forever.

And like the spring, grace descends suddenly and without warning - except, of course, that it was always coming. Its showers saturate my soul, and my thirsty ache, the cold, the loneliness - it all drains away. *You,* I remember. *How could I forget?*

Yet somehow, I have, yet again, in this winter. I've mistaken dormancy for death.

MAMA PRAYS

The child is not dead, You say, *only sleeping.* And You say it with a smile.

Lord, how can You smile at me? I see the bareness of my soul and feel defeated. There's no green here. Not a single blossom and certainly not any fruit. All I have left are roots. Roots reaching deeply, taking nourishment from good soil, soil tilled at Your direction. The rich loam of Your Body sustains me.

The branches are bare, but it is spring, and my roots run deep. Deep enough that Your call resonates through my bones, "*Talitha Koum*! Little girl, I say to You arise!"

You smile because You know that I need the winter to learn to trust, to return to my roots, to rely on You to bring back the spring. You smile because You made both for me - the chill of the winter and the vibrancy of spring.

As the air warms at Your hand, it is not only the flowers that yawn open, but my soul as well. "I'm here, Lord," I respond, "And ready to bloom."

MAMA PRAYS

22 WAILING FOR WAFFLES

My toddler eats a waffle for breakfast every morning. Despite that I have never failed to feed him, he inevitably wails for the entire two minutes it takes to pop up from the toaster. I sing and dance, trying to distract him. I explain that the waffle needs to cook. Nothing helps; the waiting is too painful.

There will come a day when the wailing stops. He will grow in patience enough to pass those moments in peace. He will trust that I, his mother, have good things in store for him, that I have reasons for taking my time, that the promised waffle will come.

It seems so silly, the intensity of his tears and the look of desperation on his face. It's hard not to laugh; some days I do. But then I wonder, is this what God sees when he looks at us in our impatience? Do we wail and despair over something He's already promised us, something that's already brewing?

Human beings are not adept at waiting.

In some ways, I wonder if this season of Advent is just a microcosm of our earthly lives. We rush around preparing for Christmas, and we get so off course. We allow menial things to overwhelm us. We lost sight of the purpose of this season: God's Kingdom - already, and not yet.

Life *is* a preparation for Heaven, and in that sense, our entire lives are a season of waiting. We are waiting for the fullness and joy God has promised us, and in the scheme of eternity, our lives are a very short time to wait. But *how* are we waiting? Are we trying to rush past the here and now, always onto the next?

I read recently that *im*patience ages us at a cellular level, which is actually kind of impressive, if you think about it. Our will to inhabit in the next moment literally pushes our cells into to theirs. But impatience is incompatible with joy.

The gift of patience is that it allows us to sink into the present moment, to absorb what's there. We can marinate in what surrounds us in the here and now. So, when we think about our lives as preparation for eternity, what is it that we want to marinate in? I wonder if looked at the ways we spend our time and the attitudes those practices cultivate, what will we find? The more we spend our small budget of time marinating in those things that make us more loving, more prayerful, and more present, the more likely it is that our souls will carry those flavors into eternity.

It's true that there are some things over which we have no control. Suffering is a reality that touches us all. But it strikes me that even in painful times, there is always something beautiful. If we can trust God enough to say "yes" to the trials of the moment, we can begin to taste and see his goodness in these, too, and develop a taste for unexpected and more complex flavors.

Thankfully, Isaiah tells us, "Blessed are *all* who wait for the Lord," (30:18d). Not just the patient or unwaveringly faithful. All. That's good news for those of us whose hearts ache with the pain of waiting.

But – I have to ask myself – *am* I waiting for the Lord? How often do I hear the news and rue the state of the world? Do I not believe Jesus's promise of his coming Kingdom enough to maintain hope? How often do I live as though my day-to-day, the concerns of this moment, is *all* there is?

How might my life look differently if I returned more often to this vision of my life as the waiting room for eternity?

This season is a reminder to each of us to live for what we already know is coming. To embrace the joy of the present moment as we anticipate and prepare for the greater joy of what's to come.

We don't need to rush; the next thing will come.

And it will come whether we've received the gift of the present moment, or not.

23 MULTIPLY ME

Everyone is crying.

Multiply me, Lord.

The house is a wreck and messes grow like weeds, faster than I can tend to them.

Multiply me, Lord.

It's need after need after need and when do I rest?

When did you rest?

MAMA PRAYS

You went away up the mountain for a moment of peace, and they followed you. Your heart wasn't bitter with frustration and you didn't sigh in exasperation at their constant neediness. Your eyes didn't well with tears like water leaving a wrung out sponge, leaving you dry, stiff, and cracked.

Your heart, Matthew says, was moved with pity.

Well, Lord, I am not you in this story.

I am the bread. The dried out, crusty leftovers without a prayer of fulfilling the needs of the crowd. My crowd is small, Lord, but they are hungry. Hungry for loving arms to reassure them, for smiles to encourage them, for eyes to witness small feats with wonder, for arms to wrap safety around them.

My body is tired and weak. "I am not enough," I want to say ten times a day. *Lord, multiply me,* I pray.

I pray wondering when grace will kick in, until I realize it isn't coming.

It's already here.

Multiply me. What does this prayer mean?

MAMA PRAYS

It means being broken and given. This is my body given for you. This is my life given for you. No one takes it from me. I lay it down for these sweet, beautiful faces and impossibly soft skin. I lay it down for the wonder that they are, and the privilege to watch them grow. This deafening chaos is my gift to savor in the present moment. The stretching and the breaking - these *are* the answers to my pleas.

It is all too much and I am not enough. My not-enoughness makes room, provides the space for me to cry to you, to place myself in your hands. It is here I am broken bit by bit. It is your hand that gives me away, and it is for me to trust the mystery of your love that distributes me. In your hands I become so much more than what I am. I am given and given and given away, and in the end, so much more than what I once was is leftover.

I am not enough. I'm not meant to be.

Multiply me, Lord.

MAMA PRAYS

24 MOTHERHOOD, OR WHY I'M STILL IN MY PAJAMAS

It's been one of those mornings. Actually, it's the afternoon now, so I guess it started out as just a morning, but it got bold as it gained strength and it's threatening to take over the whole day. It's one of those days when being a mom has meant a whole lot of momming, and not much else. Hugs, tears, tantrums, refused naps, refused meals, macaroni on the floor, cuddle time on the couch, Candyland, four rounds with the same story. All in my pajamas.

I wish I didn't feel so frustrated when the day doesn't go as planned.

I wish I didn't feel so defeated when all I accomplish in a day is...the only thing worth

MAMA PRAYS

accomplishing. Isn't this *why* I'm home? To be the one loving my kids all day long?

Instead, I feel defeated because the dishes aren't done, the laundry is *still* in the dryer, and I didn't get to finish that piece I was planning on writing because naptime didn't happen.

And I feel so alone in the middle of all of it.

But I am not alone.

I am one of many called throughout history to the mission of motherhood, and this the reality of life in the trenches.

We are the ones called to love Jesus in the least of these, in our little ones. We are the ones called to die to our egos, to the need for a sense of accomplishment. We are the Marthas, busy with many things, called to set them all aside when we hear his voice.

"Mommy, can I sit on your lap?"

"Mommy, will you read me a story?"

"Mommy, I'm hungry."

MAMA PRAYS

Can you hear him? He's calling.

MAMA PRAYS

25 LOVE IN A PILE OF SHOES

All of my shoes have been removed from my closet. They now sit in a pile at the foot of bed. My toddler, shoe relocation engineer, beams up at me with pride, handing me the last remaining shoe.

And I'm surprised by what I feel. Not frustration about the mess, or preoccupation with the burden of bending my 7-months-pregnant self over to put them all back again. No, this morning grace whispers in my ear, and all I feel is the tenderness of a God who has spent years watching me pile shoes at his feet. "This is what you want, right, God? Let me help! Let me do it."

Looking back on years of ministry, it's easy to see

the mistakes, all the things I would have done differently. I've sometimes lamented lost opportunities, thinking "if only." What might have been if I'd prayed more, been more attentive, let God lead?

And then I look at my son and his big accomplishment for the day – helping Mommy put on her shoes. He makes real to me what I already know but am invited to learn time and again: the gladness of God's heart is not in what I accomplish for him, but in the joy of my offering to Him.

I am his beloved, not his employee. His love does not correspond to the height of the offerings I lay before him. It just is.

By the end of my life, I may contribute little to God's actual mission for his kingdom, despite my high estimation of my own efforts. How freeing to know that was never the call; God doesn't need help to put on his shoes.

It is His delight simply to watch us try.

26 THIS IS MY BODY

"This is my body, given up for you."

Morning sickness. Heartburn. Backache. Sciatica. Weight gain. Labor. Stretch marks. Nursing. Everything I am, given for you. Sleepless nights, given for you. Anxiety, worry, arms holding you all night in illness. Every waking moment, given for you.

My thoughts are not my own anymore. My time is not my own. And my body is beyond the recognition of my childless self. Then again, so am I.

"In order for something greater to grow, something

lesser has to die." This is the first rule of the spiritual life, according to a dear friend and trusted advisor. A man who knows and loves Jesus like I one day hope to. This principle has certainly held true in motherhood.

The act of being a mother has transformed me. Choosing to give of myself, again and again, for the sake of my children, has slowly transformed me into someone who is less selfish and more generous. Things I used to merely pretend to want to do, I now offer with genuine joy. The refiner's fire has burned away so much of who I used to be. What's left behind is something much more like the person I always wanted to be.

Physically, the transformation has been generally a negative one. And what a trap it is for me to dwell on! To dismiss this struggle is to belittle a genuine struggle. The desire of a woman to be beautiful is not inherently a superficial one. It's written into our nature. My desire to be alluring to my husband is not trivial. The trap I fall into is that the ways I try to address this desire miss the mark.

St. Augustine believed that at the final Resurrection, we will all rise in perfected bodies – all except the martyrs, who will retain their wounds, wounds that will be beautiful. I wonder – will my stretch marks be beautiful?

MAMA PRAYS

"This is my body, given up for you." The phrase crosses my mind often when pondering the mystery of early motherhood. Even "easy" pregnancies are exhausting. As a nursing mother, my body continues to provide the sustenance that my son needs – everything that he takes in that becomes his own body. In so many ways, my body is no longer my own. My arms are safety. My kiss is comfort. My kneeling form, bent over weeding the garden is a jungle gym. My eyes are essential, my gaze required for so many new dances and tricks to a chorus of, "Mommy, watch what I can do!"

I suppose as they grow, I will continue to see new ways in which this body will be offered up for the ones I love. Time will paint lines on my face from so many smiles and nights spent worrying. My hands will resemble my mother's hands, and then my grandmother's hands. So many changes, and what a trap it will be to dwell on them. My body, my life, is not a gift given to me to preen over and bathe in self-adulation. I was made to be poured out, offered up, and given away.

I hope I do just that. Amid so many competing desires – some holy, others less so – it is so easy to flit from attending one to the other without really considering where the desire comes from, or who it ultimately serves. That can all become so hazy. I suppose the only way to clarity is to check in with Jesus often. When my life on earth comes to a close, when this body last draws breath, I hope I will have

MAMA PRAYS

given it in service. I hope I will have spent my time
on the good and the beautiful. Lord, make it so.
This is my body, given for You.

27 COME OUT OF YOUR HIDING PLACE

My daughter eats crayons. She is a crayon eater. In the past, it has been just a nibble here, or a bite there. This time, I came out of my son's nursery to discover her hiding under her toddler-sized table, crayon wrappers littered about.

"Why are you hiding?"

"Because I did something bad."

"Did you eat your crayon?" A nod. I search for the remnants.

MAMA PRAYS

"Did you eat your *whole* crayon?"

Still laying under her table, her favorite place to wallow in guilt, she looks everywhere but my face and holds up two fingers.

"You ate *two* crayons?" Now, I am impressed. From nibble upon nibble, she acquired a taste and had graduated from a waxy *amuse bouche* to full-blown Crayola feast.

That's how sin works, isn't it?

Bit by bit, inch by inch, nibble by nibble, we acquire the taste of something we know is forbidden until it feels like we can't say no. We'd rather hide under the table, feasting on filth, then to come back into the light.

Even when we are caught in our sin and admit what we've done wrong, even when we hear the Father calling to us to come out, that sinking feeling of shame slithers out of the darkness and wraps around, tightening its hold on us.

Today, that hold is broken. There is no hiding from Christ. Come out from shame and darkness. Whatever your sin, give it to Christ on the cross. There's nothing he isn't up there for. He wants it all. Don't hold back. He's waiting.

MAMA PRAYS

28 LOOK INTO THE FACE OF LOVE

"I'm sorry, Mommy!" My toddler said these words repeatedly after having shattered a teacup she'd been playing with. She was so distraught. I wanted to comfort her and tell her it was alright, that we could fix it, and more importantly, that I wasn't upset with her. I knew the teacup might break if she played with it, and I gave it to her anyway. To me, it was worth the risk so that she could have the joy of playing with it. I had expected the teacup to eventually end up in pieces; I hadn't anticipated how ashamed she would be of breaking it. Her expectations of herself were higher than mine of her. "I'm sorry, Mommy," she kept repeating. All I wanted was to take her little face in my hands, look her in the eyes, and tell her I loved her. But she

MAMA PRAYS

wouldn't look up.

"Look at me, little one." She was so afraid that she kept her face hidden. "I'm sorry, Mommy." My heart ached for her to look up at my face, to look into my eyes so that she would see what I felt for her in that moment. Not anger, not even impatience. Only a desire to love her, to put my arms around her and to comfort her.

God was offering me a glimpse of what he feels for us when we turn away from him in moments of fear, of shame, of self-loathing. The isolation of sin is self-imposed. If only we would turn to God, we would see the face of love. Like the father in the story of the prodigal son, he waits and watches for us to come to home. Our capacity to receive his mercy is contingent only on our own willingness to turn and embrace it.

The Psalmist says, "Let us see your face and we will be saved." To look into the face of God is to look into the face of love, and to know that ultimately nothing we could ever do can separate us from the love of God.

29 STAY WITH ME

It's quiet in the dark, except for the screaming. I hold my one-year-old, skin hot from fever, as he writhes against me. "No, no" he cries, little hands trying to force me away. He wants neither down nor up. I'm used to being the touch that soothes - a useless gift when everything hurts.

My back aches from bearing his weight on top of my own, ligaments shifting with the expansion of my pregnant form. I wish I could offer him the comfort of nursing, but the pain of a baby who bites on top of the tenderness of pregnancy is too much. Conflicting forces rise inside me - the desire to stop him, the guilt that follows, and the tiny, rational part of me that reassures me it's okay.

"I'm not asking for it to not be hard," I pray, "I just don't want to feel so alone."

And suddenly, I'm not. My Mother is there with me, and together we hold our sons in their pain. These moments in the darkness will pass. The pain will be forgotten - the pain, but not the lesson. This is the gift of all mothers, to sit together as we hold hurts and patch wounds we cannot heal. We bear witness when the only gift we have is that of our presence.

Being there. That's it. We have no power to change anything. Except, of course, that being there changes everything. Anyone who's ever suffered knows that mere suffering is not the same as suffering alone. The light of a single flame, however small, is enough to soften the darkness.

And so, Mary sits with me. Mary, and Gianna, and Zelie, and Dorothy - all the holy mothers who have come before me. This is our treasure to share in, to insist on the power of love when love seems powerless. To be present in the darkness and know, even when we cannot see it, that our presence brings light to that darkness.

30 VIA DOLOROSA

Do I love you enough to let you suffer? This road you walk is a painful one. Each of your wounds I feel in my own body. How, why, Lord, does it have to be this way?

I know that this is the way of life. Some gates only open by way of suffering. What waits on the other side: light, beauty, redemption. Your suffering is not without meaning and purpose. But what it costs me to watch you pass through it.

This is for good, I remind myself when I want to reach out and intervene. This trial, this setting of bone, this heartbreak, this long, slow march to

MAMA PRAYS

Calvary. Am I strong enough to stay by your side, even through this?

I want to take your pain and make it my own. But - what would that leave you?

Sheltered from pain and struggle, a limp butterfly with wet, crumpled wings, grounded forever. It is the crucible of escaping the chrysalis on your own that frees you to take flight. So I watch you fight this battle on your own. Watch, and pray.

Mary and I stand shoulder to shoulder, watching our babies march through the wickedness of this world. We watch, we pray, we trust you to your Father. In this mystery that is motherhood, you were never truly ours. It is we who are yours. The suffering we've born for you we would gladly embrace all again. And so, this too, we accept. The swords of your pain pierce our hearts, and with each beat we bleed. We accept this pain as you accept your cross. We hold it close, our last-resort love.

We've given you everything we have to give. This, you must do on your own. Take our love and our lessons. Suffer well.

I will, like Mary, stand watch until it's over, and hold you when it ends.

MAMA PRAYS

ABOUT THE AUTHOR

Samantha Stephenson is a Catholic wife and homeschooling mama of four, host of the podcasts "Brave New Us" and "Mama Prays," and author of *Reclaiming Motherhood from a Culture Gone Mad*. She holds master's degrees in theology and bioethics and her writing has been featured at Blessed Is She, CatholicMom.com, Crisis Magazine, FemCatholic, Notre Dame's Grotto Network, and Our Sunday Visitor. Follow her blog at MamaPrays.com or sign up for her newsletter at www.FaithandBioethics.com to receive the latest updates on medical research, technology, and culture.